LOOK IT UP
Now in a fully revised edition
1. You and Your Body
2. People and Customs
3. What People Do
4. The Prehistoric World
5. Ships and Boats
6. People of Long Ago
7. The Sea
8. The Earth
9. Cold-Blooded Animals
10. Warm-Blooded Animals
11. Sport and Entertainment
12. The World of Machines
13. Land Travel
14. Flying
15. Outer Space
16. Index

Photo Credits: British Tourist Authority; Douglas Dickins, F.R.P.S.; Jonathan Eastland; Robert Harding Associates; Michael Holford; Leo Mason; Overseas Containers Ltd.; Picturepoint; Shell Oil; ZEFA.

Front cover: ZEFA.

Illustrators: Fred Anderson; John Sibbick; John Barber; Andrew Skilleter; John Bilham; George Thompson; Jacky Cowdrey; Chris Flynn; Gilchrist Studios; Elizabeth Graham-Yool; Colin Hawkins; Richard Hook; Illustra; Eric Jewell; Angus McBride; Ann Procter; Mike Roffe.

First edition © Macmillan Publishers Limited, 1979
Reprinted in 1981, 1982, 1983 and 1984
Second edition © Macmillan Publishers Limited, 1985

All rights reserved. No reproduction, copy or transmission of this publication in any form or by any means, may be made without written permission

Chief Educational Adviser
Lynda Snowdon

Teacher Advisory Panel
Helen Craddock, John Enticknap, Arthur Razzell

Editorial Board
Jan Burgess, Rosemary Canter, Philip M. Clark, Beatrice Phillpotts, Sue Seddon, Philip Steele

Picture Researchers
Caroline Adams, Anne Marie Ehrlich, Gayle Hayter, Ethel Hurwicz, Pat Hodgson, Stella Martin, Frances Middlestorb

Designer
Keith Faulkner

Contributors and consultants
John E. Allen, Neil Ardley, Sue Becklake, Robert Burton, Barry Cox, Jacqueline Dineen, David J. Fletcher, Plantagenet Somerset Fry, Bill Gunston, Robin Kerrod, Mark Lambert, Anne Millard, Kaye Orten, Ian Ridpath, Peter Stephens, Nigel Swann, Aubrey Tulley, Tom Williamson, Thomas Wright

Published by Macmillan Children's Books
a division of Macmillan Publishers Limited
4 Little Essex Street, London WC2R 3LF
Associated companies throughout the world

ISBN 0 333 39723 1 (volume 5)
ISBN 0 333 39568 9 (complete set)

Printed in Hong Kong

Ships and Boats

Second Edition
LOOK IT UP

Contents

	Page
SMALL BOATS	**4**
The first boats	6
Simple craft today	8
RIVERS AND CANALS	**10**
Voyage by river	12
How a canal works	14
Canals	16
SAILING SHIPS	**18**
Oars and sails	20
Galleons and cogs	22
Life on board ship	24
Clipper ships	26
Tall ships	28
Modern sailing ships	30
STEAMSHIPS	**32**
The Great Britain	34
Battleships	36

	Page
CARGO SHIPS	**38**
Modern cargo	**40**
Tankers	**42**
Shipbuilding	**44**
PASSENGER SHIPS	**46**
Liners	**47**
Ferries	**48**
Hydrofoils	**50**
Hovercraft	**51**
MODERN WARSHIPS	**52**
On a warship	**54**
Submarines	**56**
UNUSUAL SHIPS	**58**
Ships for special purposes	**60**
Record-breaking ships	**62**
DID YOU KNOW?	**64**

SMALL BOATS

Many people use small boats for pleasure. Some boats are rowed by oars or paddles. Some have sails, which are arranged in many different ways. Other kinds of boats have engines. People learn all about boats before they go on the water.

sailing boat

windsurfer

speed boat

fishing boat

houseboat

Most of these small boats are too big to take home. They are kept in riverside boathouses, on big lakes, or in sea harbours. Inflatable boats can be taken home. All the air is let out of them first.

The first boats

People learned to float down rivers on logs long before they could ride horses or make carts. This man is going on a hunting trip. He has two logs tied together to support him. He paddles along with his hands. His spear is tied on to the logs.

Stone-age people made better boats, called 'dug-outs'. They hollowed out tree trunks. They used fire and stone axes to do this.

This man is standing on a raft made of tree trunks lashed together. His paddle helps him to steer his boat where he wants to go.

This fine sailing ship was built about five thousand years ago. The float, fixed to poles called outriggers, stopped it from blowing over.

float

Simple craft today

The largest Chinese boats are called junks. They have a flat bottom, a blunt front, the bow, and a high back, the stern.

We can see all these boats on the water today. They have been made in the same way for hundreds of years. Now boats are beginning to be made differently. There are new ways of using metals and plastics.

In large areas of South America the jungle is thick and dangerous. There are no roads, so people travel along the great rivers. This longboat is used in Peru.

This picture was taken in Hong Kong. Here the land is overcrowded, and many thousands of people live on board boats.

Coracles are small one-man boats. They have a cover of stretched skin and are light enough to be carried. They are used in Wales for fishing.

Many of the simplest boats are made of bundles of reeds tied together. This reed boat is sailing on Lake Titicaca in South America.

RIVERS AND CANALS

Canals are waterways made by man. They are straighter than rivers, and wide enough for boats to pass each other easily. Most canals were made 150 years ago, when roads were bad and few railways had been built.

Long ago horses were used to drag along heavy loads. It often took as many as six horses to pull one cart.

The picture below shows tugs and barges on the Rhine in Germany. There is more river traffic on the Rhine than on any other river in the world. Goods from factories and mines nearby are sent by river.

When a canal was built the same heavy loads were put on a barge. This was pulled by just one horse.

Sometimes rivers and canals go in different ways to reach a town. The river flows along the lowest part of the land. The canal may cross over the river as this one does. It goes over a kind of bridge.

Voyage by river

The Egyptians built boats like this five thousand years ago. This boat is on the River Nile, one of the world's great rivers. The Nile flows from the south to the north of Egypt. It has always been the main transport route through Egypt.

Egyptian ships are the oldest ships we know about. Some of the earliest ships had a mast like a letter A. This ship has one mast and a long rectangular sail. The large oar at the stern was for steering.

The other boats in the picture are called galleys. They were rowed by teams of men pulling oars.

How a canal works

When a canal is built on sloping land it has to be made like a series of steps. The different levels of the steps are joined by locks. Locks are pairs of gates. When they are shut no water can get in or out. Only a few boats at a time can use the lock. Boats must wait their turn.

Locks have two pairs of gates, one at each end. The two pairs are never open at once. A boat enters through one pair of gates. Water is slowly run into or out of the lock through the sluices. The boat is then raised or lowered to the right level and leaves by the other gates.

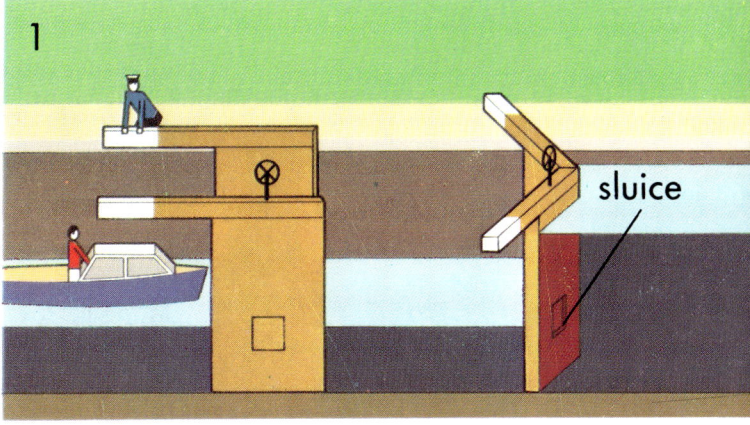

Here a boat is entering a lock from the lower level. The top gates are kept shut.

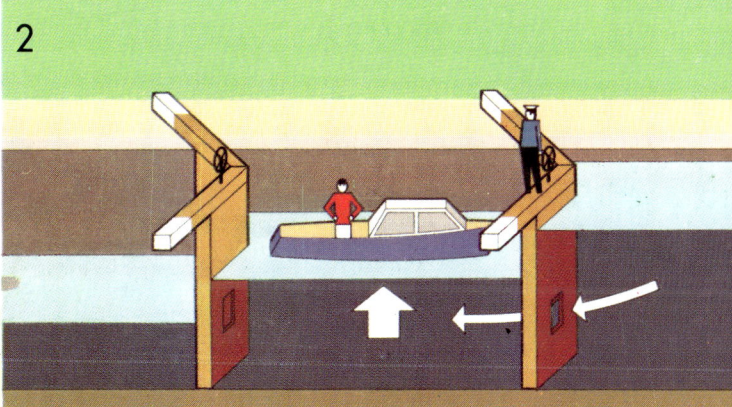

The lower gates shut. The top gate sluice gently lets in water to raise the boat. Then the top gates open.

One city with beautiful canals is Amsterdam in Holland. This boat is taking sightseers on a trip along the Prince Regent Canal.

Canals

Most canals link towns and cities but some have other uses. Sometimes canals are cut through narrow parts of land to join two seas together. Other canals are short waterways which are inside cities. They are used instead of streets.

It was hard work building canals. The men who built them were called navigators. They were later nicknamed 'navvies'.

This is the Corinth Canal in Greece. It is one of the sea canals that were cut through land to join two seas together. Sea canals made voyages much shorter. People no longer had to sail round huge continents.

Venice, in Italy, has canals instead of streets. In the old city, boats called gondolas are used instead of taxis. They take people where they want to go. Some people in Venice even need a boat to visit their next door neighbours!

SAILING SHIPS

Thousands of years ago men learned that a ship could be driven along by the wind pushing against a sail.

At first sailing ships could only go where the wind blew them.
Then new types of sail were invented that could be swung from side to side. Now men could use the wind from all directions and sail anywhere. To go directly into the wind they had to go in a zig-zag. This process is called tacking.

Modern sails are curved. The wind blows over the curve and lifts the sail. Blow over the top of a piece of paper. Watch the paper lifting.

When a boat tacks in a strong wind the crew have to lean out as far as they can. This stops the boat from being blown over. On each tack they have to change sides.

No one should go sailing without learning how to swim and how to sail. In Germany there are special schools to teach young sailing crews how to sail properly.

A thousand years ago Vikings from Northern seas sailed in ships like this. They sailed across the Atlantic Ocean. They also raided Britain.

Oars and sails

Galleys were large ships rowed by many men. They moved much faster than ships that had sails but no oars. When there was no wind, sailing ships without oars hardly moved at all. Pirates preferred to use galleys. Since galleys moved faster, pirates could overtake sailing ships.

The Arabs invented the lateen sail a thousand years ago. Their boats could go across or into the wind.

lateen sail

This interesting Greek galley is very like Egyptian ships built five thousand years ago. It has a sail and a pointed metal bow to smash into enemy ships. There are two banks of oars, so this galley is called a bireme. Some galleys had several more rows of oars. The soldiers had shields to protect them.

Galleons and cogs

About six hundred years ago most ships had sails but no oars. Galleons were the largest ships. They had three or four masts rigged with many large sails. Cogs were simple cargo ships with wide hulls and one mast.

At the top of the mast was a place called the crow's-nest. A sailor in the crow's-nest kept a look-out for land, or for other ships.

Men on ships had to fight pirates. Their ships had high decks at each end. They fought from there.

By about five hundred years ago merchant ships were able to make long voyages. National flags had been invented. They were flown at the tops of the masts.

Life on board ship

In the old days there were no tinned foods and no fridges. Crews often became ill because they had no fresh vegetables or fruit to eat. The sea was too salty to drink and there was little fresh water.

Life on board the old sailing ships was hard. Voyages often took a year. The sailors were often cross and unhappy. They were cramped together and the work was tiring. Fights and arguments broke out.

The hardest and most dangerous work was hauling up the sails and letting them down. Men had to climb rope ladders to the top of the tall masts to pull up the sails.

Sailors had to climb the masts in dreadful storms. The ship tossed from side to side and the ropes and sails flapped about.

When a galleon met a severe gale her sails had to be taken down. A strong wind could snap the masts or tear the sails to shreds.

In the old days crews slept either on the hard deck or in a hammock. A hammock was a bed of netting or canvas. It was unrolled each night and slung from a hook at each end. Hammocks were quite comfortable.

When heavy ropes had to be pulled they were fixed to a capstan. A capstan was like a drum with poles sticking out like the spokes of a wheel. The capstan turned as the men pushed the poles round. They sang songs called sea shanties to help them work together in time.

Many clipper ships had figureheads to bring luck. These were carved figures fixed to the bows.

Clipper ships

Clipper ships were the fastest sailing ships. They raced across the world with cargoes of tea and other goods. They were big ships and had several masts. Each mast was fully rigged with sails. Clipper ships needed a large crew.

One of the most famous clippers to be built was named Cutty Sark. You can see it in the picture on the right. It still exists. It is on the River Thames at Greenwich, in England.

The clipper ships Taeping and Ariel once had a race from Foochow in China to England. This was well over a hundred years ago. Everybody got excited about fast ships and their races just as today people are excited about football.

Tall ships

Large sailing ships that carried cargoes about a hundred years ago are called tall ships. There were two kinds of tall ships, barques and schooners. Barques usually had three masts and schooners had two. Both barques and schooners had lots of sails. A few tall ships are used today for training.

This is a training school sailing ship. It has three masts and lots of sails. It is a barque.

rope ladder

Life on a modern training ship is often as tough and as dangerous as in the old days. Young sailors have to climb up the rigging to roll up or unroll the great sails. They have to work in all kinds of weather.

Viking boat

medieval ship

Modern sailing ships

Most of today's sailing ships are used for sport. Nearly all of them are small. They do not go very far from land. A few of the bigger sailing ships are used for ocean racing. There are even races for sailing ships that go round the world.

Life on an ocean racer is exciting. The crew know a lot about sailing and work well together.

This boat is called a yawl. It has a huge front sail called a spinnaker. Spinnakers increase the boat's speed.

barque

modern sailing boat

Sails have changed a lot over two thousand years. At first ships were made to go faster by adding more masts and sails. Today racers seldom have more than one mast. They sail the fastest of all!

One of the world's record-breaking racers is called Crossbow. It does have more than one mast. It has two hulls, side by side, with a mast on each hull.

31

medieval sailing boat

schooner

paddle steamer

The Great Eastern 1858

Mauretania 1907

Steamships developed gradually from sailing ships. For many years they kept their sails because their engines often broke down. Steamships gave up sails about 100 years ago.

STEAMSHIPS

All the earliest steamships had paddle wheels. There was usually one on each side of the ship.

Paddle wheels were like old water wheels. But instead of being driven round by the flow of water, they were driven round by the engines. The wheels pushed the sea water behind them.

The sternwheeler had a wheel at the back. It was used on rivers too narrow for ships with paddle wheels. This one is Canadian.

This paddle steamer is in Disneyworld in America. It is a copy of a steamship used 100 years ago. It was used on the Mississippi River.

The Great Britain

This ship was designed by a famous engineer called Brunel. He also built some of Britain's great railways and bridges. The Great Britain was finished in 1843.

The Great Britain was the biggest ship in the world. Other ships were made of wood but the Great Britain was made of iron. It had a screw propeller which was a new invention. The ship is now in Bristol, England.

Battleships

For a long time armoured battleships were the biggest warships. They carried heavy guns. The first time they were used in battle was in 1866. It was during a war between Italy and Austria.

swivelling turrets

In 1906 the Dreadnought was designed and made in Britain. It was the first battleship to have its large guns fitted in swivelling turrets. These turrets allowed the guns to fire to the left or to the right. The design of the Dreadnought surprised everyone.

Other countries copied Dreadnought. Many giant battleships were built.

They were not used very often after World War Two. Navies normally used other kinds of ships.

One of the last battleships was the USS Alabama. It was built at the end of World War Two. Since 1982 America has begun to put some back in use.

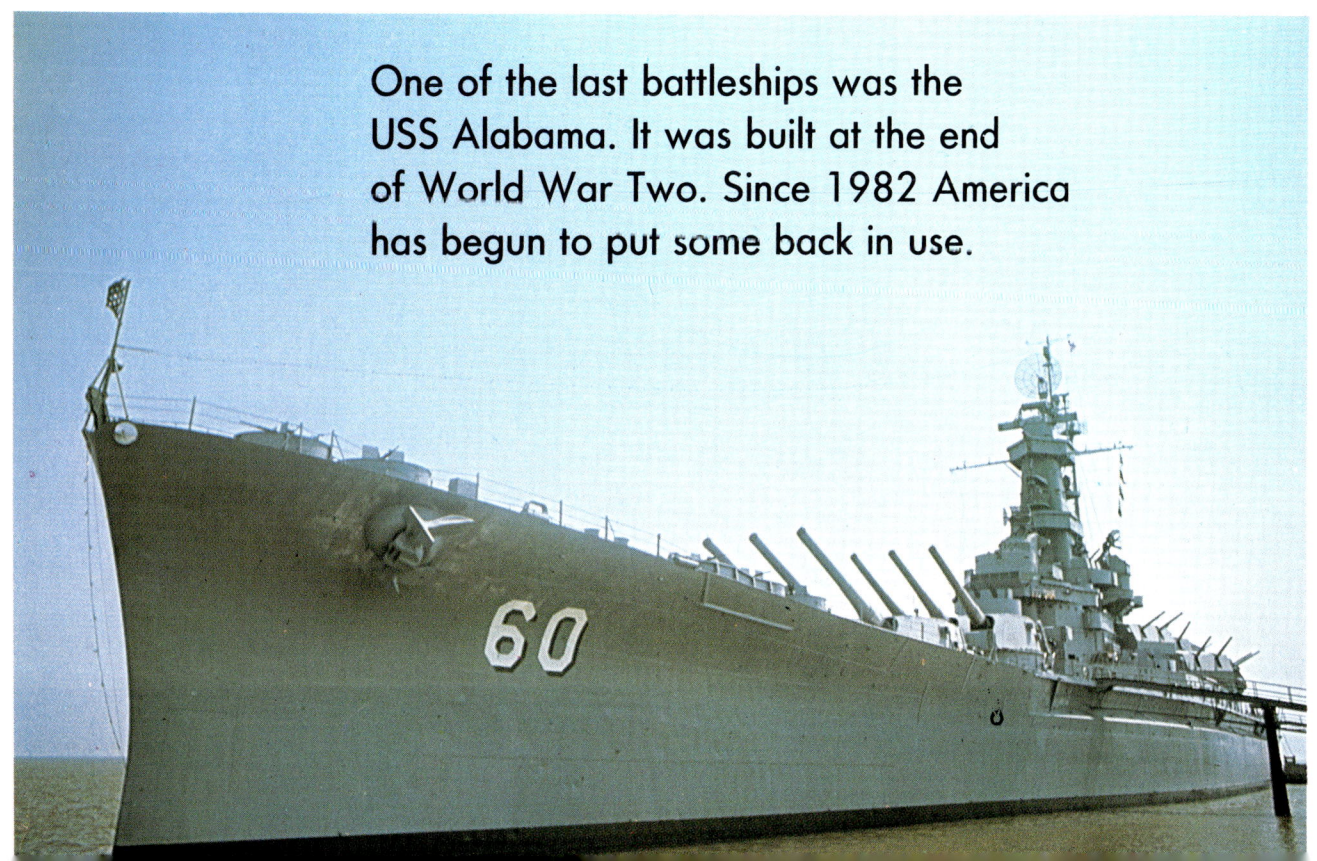

CARGO SHIPS

Several hundred years ago ships took people from Europe to settle in North America. The same ships brought back lots of different goods from America to Europe. The cargoes included things like potatoes and tobacco. These goods had never been seen before in Europe.

In the old days cargo included many different things. Barrels of flour, barrels of wine, live animals and carcases of meat, coils of rope and stacks of timber were all mixed up together. It took a long time to load and unload the boxes, barrels, crates and loose cargo such as coal and gravel. It was very tiring work.

Modern cargo

Today the way of moving cargo has changed. Ships carry either bulk or container cargo. Coal and oil are bulk cargoes. They are poured into the hold or sucked out at great speed by machines. Other kinds of cargo such as furniture, books, radios, pens and cars are all packed into large containers.

Grain, such as wheat, oats, barley and rye, does not have to be put into sacks. It is loaded and unloaded through great pipes.

Coffee is usually packed in sacks. Cranes move large numbers of the sacks at the same time.

Containers are designed to fit exactly into certain parts of ships, trains, trucks and cargo aircraft.

The most important bulk cargo is oil. It travels in special ships. These ships are called tankers.

Tankers

During the past hundred years tankers have increased in size and number. Today they are the biggest ships in the world. They have grown in size because the bigger the tanker the more cheaply it carries each tonne of oil. Bulk carriers have cabins and funnels at the back of the ship. All the goods are stored together.

navigating bridge

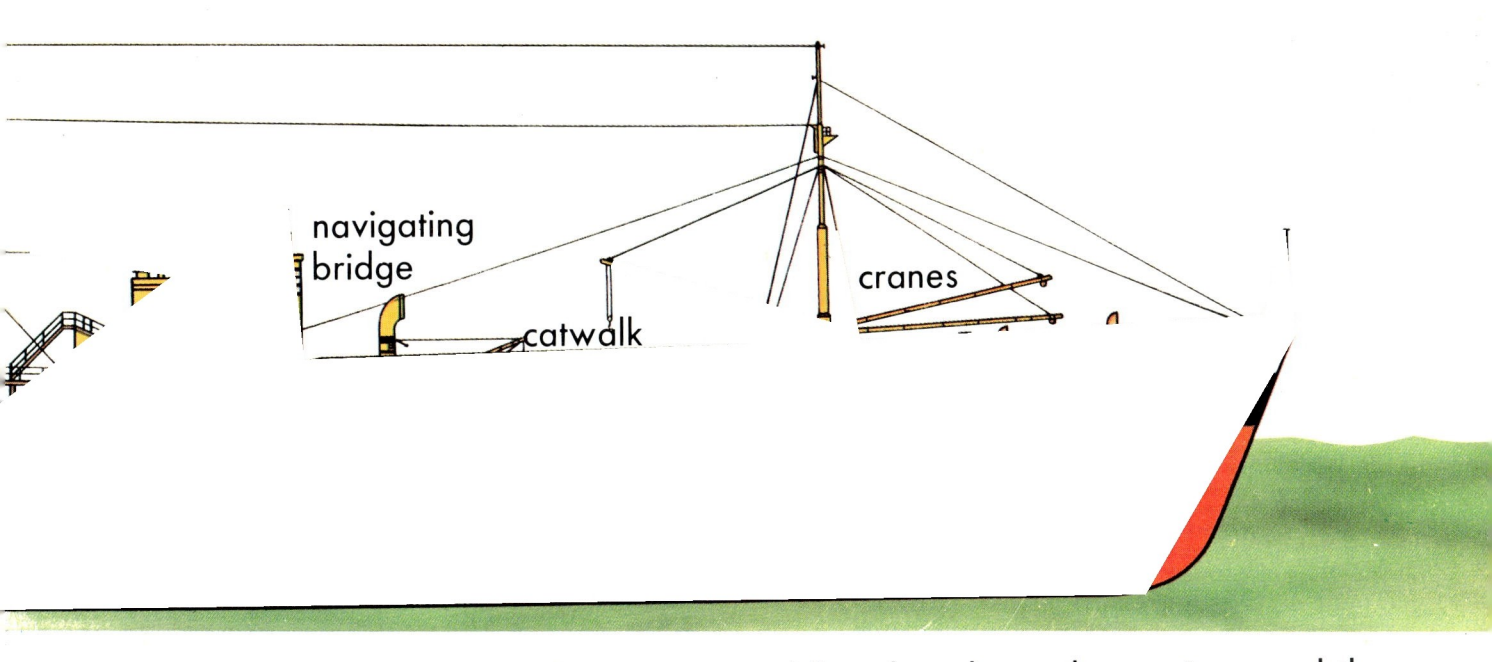

catwalk

cranes

All tankers have the engines and the crew's cabins at the stern. Some tankers have a navigating bridge about half-way along the ship.

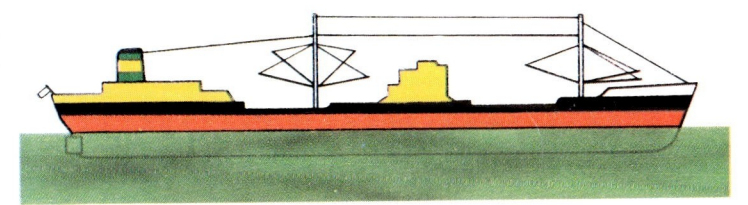

When its tanks are empty the tanker rides high, with most of its great hull out of the water.

A tanker's hull is usually painted in two colours. The part above the water is grey or black and the underside is red.

On the biggest tankers the crew use bicycles to go from one part of the deck to another. On some tankers it takes twenty minutes to walk from the bow to the stern.

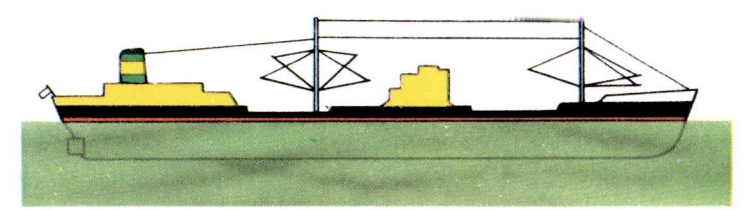

A fully laden tanker is like an iceberg. There is more under the surface of the water than on top.

Shipbuilding

Today the biggest ships are prefabricated. Large parts are made in a factory. They are put into place by a giant crane and welded in position. This makes the outdoor work quicker. The rest of the work is done in a warm factory.

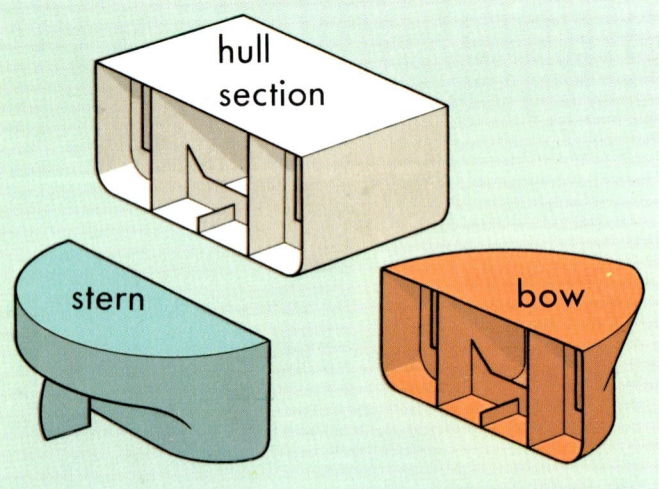

Some builders use the same kind of bow and stern for all their ships. The hull sections are the same, too.

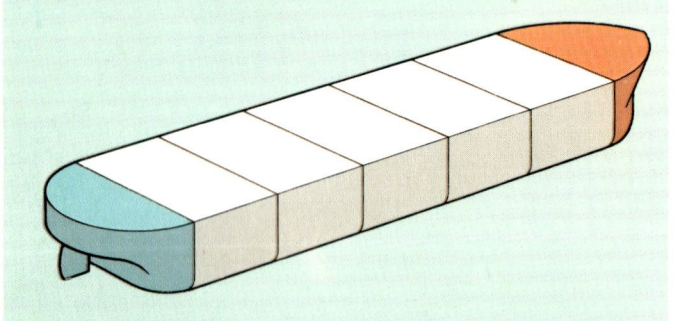

The sections are welded together in the right order to make a complete ship. It may take only a few months to make a ship from start to finish.

44

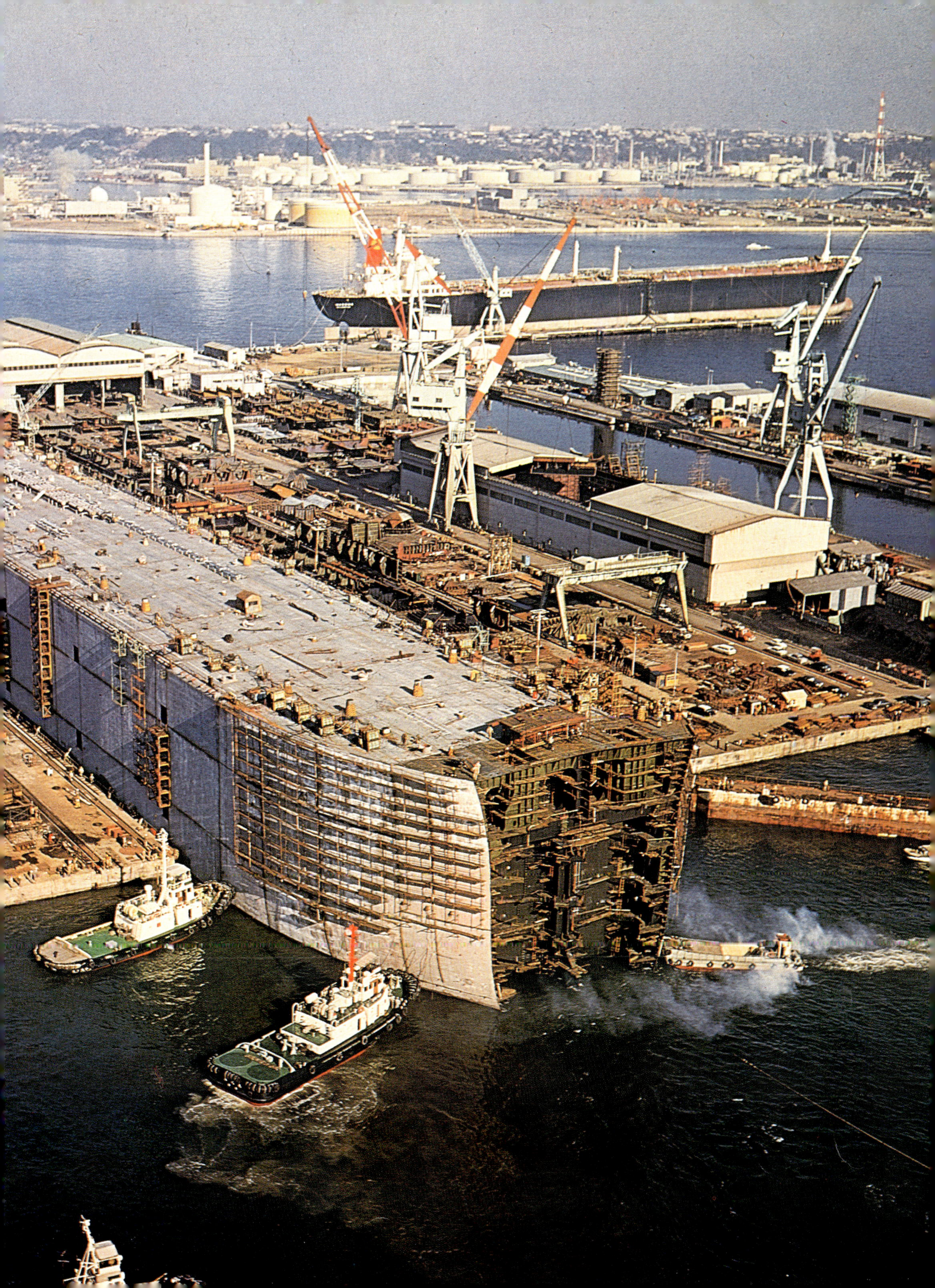

PASSENGER SHIPS

Liners

For many years passenger ships called liners were the only way that most people could cross the sea to different places. When people started using aeroplanes for travel, less liners were needed. Today the few liners that are left are used for cruises. They are floating holiday hotels, where everyone has a good time on board. This liner is the Queen Elizabeth the Second. People sometimes call her the QE2.

Ferries

A ferry is a boat that travels between two places that are fairly close together. Some ferries take people across a river where there is no bridge. Other ferries take people across a bay or large harbour. The fastest ferries are new kinds of ships called hydrofoils.

In Hong Kong thousands of people use the Star Ferry daily. Now that there is a new underwater tunnel many people use that instead.

Star Ferry

The smallest ferries are pulled over the river by hauling on a rope. The rope is fixed to each bank.

Ferries are particularly important where the stretch of water to be crossed is too wide for a bridge or a tunnel. Everyone has to pay to use a ferry.

Some big modern ferries are called Ro-Ro ships. Ro-Ro means Roll-on and Roll-off. You drive your car or truck straight on board. This one has the entrance under the hinged bow.

Train ferries have rails fixed to the deck. The train is carefully driven on board and off again at the destination. The train may be made up of goods wagons, or full of passengers asleep in bed!

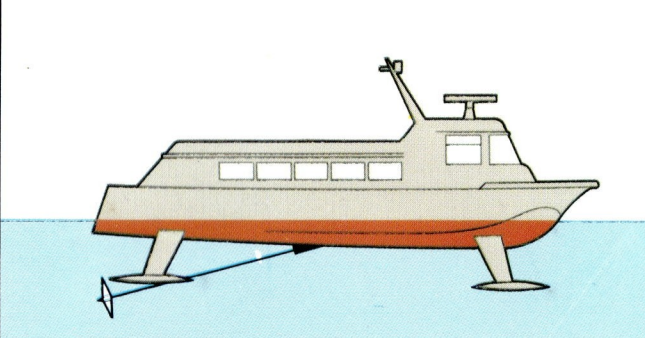

At anchor a hydrofoil rests in the water like other craft.

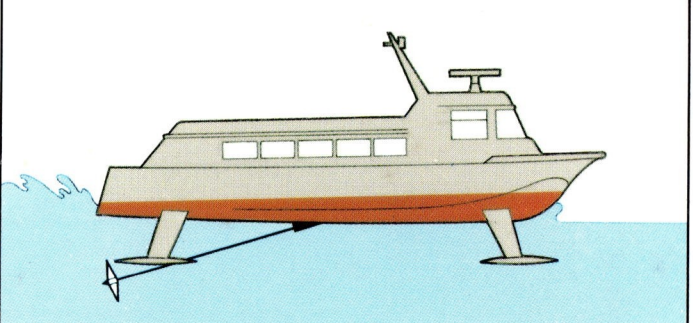

As it moves forward it begins to rise up on its lifting foils.

Hydrofoils

A hydrofoil is a boat that rides above the water. It is supported on small 'water wings' called foils. Hydrofoils can go much faster than ordinary ships, so they are useful as ferries. In a rough sea they can be steadier than other ships. Some hydrofoils can fold away the foils.

At full speed the foils keep the hull completely out of the water. Because of this, hydrofoils go very fast.

Hovercraft

These craft are sometimes called air-cushion vehicles. This is because they are supported by a cushion of air which is pumped in below. Most hovercraft are used over water but they can travel on land. They can go over soft mud, marsh and snow where no other vehicles can go.

When it isn't moving, a hovercraft can float in the water, or it can park on land.

When the engines are started the craft rises up on its cushion of air. Then it skims across the waves.

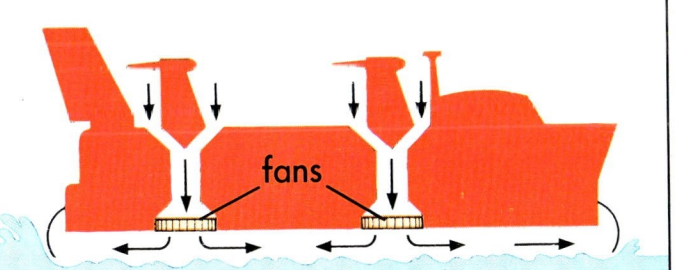

The engines drive giant fans. These fans suck in air and blow it into the cushion to keep the hovercraft up.

destroyer

MODERN WARSHIPS

Today's warships still have guns and armour like the old warships but many things are new about them. Crews of modern warships are much smaller in number. Many jobs are now done automatically by machines worked by computers.

Cruisers and destroyers are both warships. Cruisers are big ships. Destroyers are smaller but can move very fast. Both kinds of ship have lots of radar aerials.

cruiser

aircraft carrier

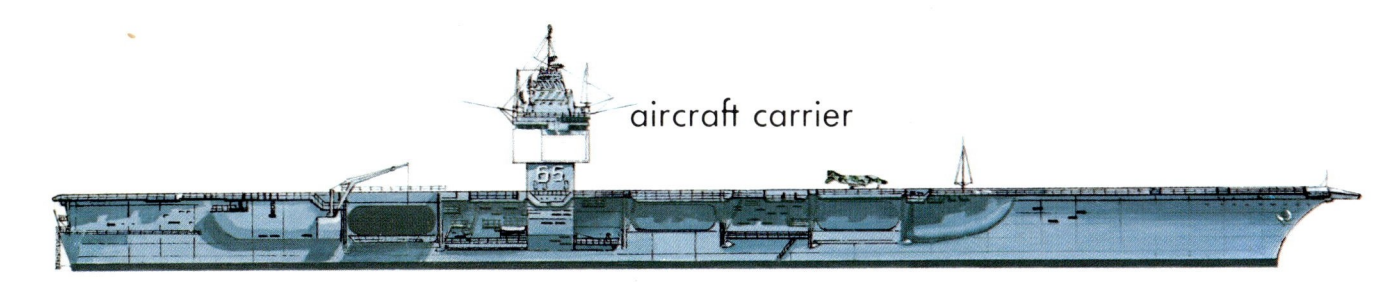

The biggest warships are aircraft carriers. These are floating bases for aircraft. Carriers can have as many as five thousand men on board.

cruiser

patrol gunboat

A few cruisers do not need funnels. They have nuclear engines. They carry missiles to hit enemy aircraft and submarines.

A new kind of ship is both a helicopter carrier and anti-submarine cruiser. This one has anti-aircraft missiles as well.

submarines

Today's nuclear-powered submarines can stay underwater for months at a time. They often carry long-range missiles that can hit enemy cities.

frigate

Frigates are useful ships that can do many jobs. They have guns and anti-aircraft or anti-submarine missiles. They usually have a helicopter, too.

53

On a warship

In the old days there were hundreds of sailors working on quite small ships. They were paid very little money. Life on board a modern warship is very different.

The captain is in charge of the ship. When he stands on the bridge he can contact any part of the ship by intercom.

At one time men worked in the engine room. It was very dirty and noisy. Today there is often nobody there at all. Someone goes down occasionally to check up.

This object is called a paravane. It is put into the sea and towed by the ship. Paravanes can blow up mines or cut them free. Minesweeping makes the seas safe for ships.

Today the crew of a warship is fairly small, but very skilled at their jobs. Much of the hard work is done by computers. Life on board is quite comfortable, but even so sailors must stay away from home for long periods.

Modern warships are fitted with radar for navigating. Radar can detect other ships and aircraft even in fog or at night. Each object shows as a spot of light on a screen.

Meals are prepared in the galley. There are no computers here but the cooks have all the things you would usually find in the kitchen of a

Submarines

Submarines are boats that travel under the surface of the water for most of the time. Early submarines drowned their inventors. By about 1900 engineers could make submarines that went to sea, dived and came up again safely.

A canvas bell was one of the first submarines. It was weighted with bags filled with lead balls. Boats joined together lowered it down.

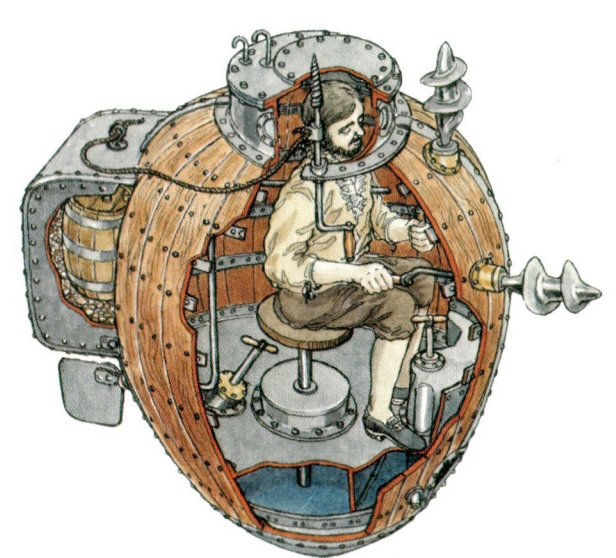

Two hundred years ago an American made a submarine called the Turtle. He used it to try to sink British ships with a barrel of explosive.

missile tubes

The biggest modern submarines are used to carry missiles. The missiles are fired out of large tubes sealed with watertight doors at the top. It looks like this in a submarine.

This American submarine is at Monte Carlo. It can travel on the surface of the water. If there was a war it would stay hidden in the sea for a long time and sink enemy ships.

Would you like to go down into the ocean in a submarine?

57

Velocipede

Velocipede

UNUSUAL SHIPS

Over the years many men have tried to invent different kinds of ships. These are some of their ideas.
The Velocipede was used in Boston, America. It was a small boat.
A man at the back pedalled it along.

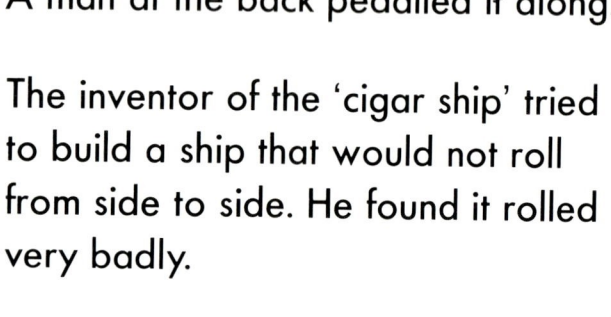

The inventor of the 'cigar ship' tried to build a ship that would not roll from side to side. He found it rolled very badly.

This Russian battleship was called Admiral Popoff. It was designed to be completely circular so that it could easily fire in any direction. It did not work properly.

The Connector was hinged so that different parts could bend up and down with the waves.

59

Ships for special purposes

There are lots of jobs that need special kinds of boats and ships to do them. One of the strangest ships is designed to tilt up on end so that the bow points straight down deep into the sea. People inside the ship can study life in the ocean.

Fire floats are used by firemen to put out fires in buildings near seas or rivers. Their powerful engines pump up the water and squirt it out through hoses at the fire.

A pontoon is a flat-bottomed boat used to support something. When a bridge has to be built in a hurry it can be supported by a row of pontoons. Armies like pontoon bridges because they are portable. They use them for crossing rivers which do not have proper bridges.

Ships for expeditions to the North or South Pole have to be made much stronger than other vessels. They have to move through thick ice.

Dredgers are ships fitted with lots of scoops on a long belt or chain. They scoop out sand and mud from the bottom of harbours or canals. The biggest ships can then move without getting stuck.

Record-breaking ships

Ships can break records in lots of ways. They can be the largest or the fastest. They can make a record-breaking voyage or dive to the greatest depth. The biggest ship of all is the tanker Seawise Giant, built in 1979. She is one thousand five hundred and four metres long.

The ship with the biggest sails was not an ordinary sailing ship. It was the battleship Temeraire. It was built a century ago. It had engines as well.

Ferdinand de Magellan of Portugal led the first expedition round the world. It took three years. He was killed on the Philippine Islands on this voyage. Only one ship and eighteen men finished the journey.

The picture on the right shows the fastest liner, called the United States. On her maiden voyage in 1952 she crossed the Atlantic at an average speed of 65 kilometres an hour.

62

The biggest warships are American nuclear-powered aircraft carriers. Twelve of them have a flight-deck 77 metres wide. They are the widest ships ever built.

Trieste has dived deeper than any other vessel. With two men inside its sphere it dived 11 kilometres in 1960.

63

DID YOU KNOW?

Fifty years ago Atlantic liners used to launch sea planes packed with urgent letters. The letters arrived long before the ships.

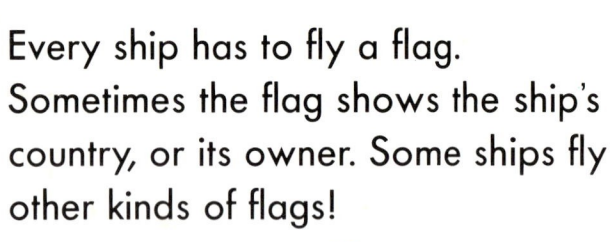

Every ship has to fly a flag. Sometimes the flag shows the ship's country, or its owner. Some ships fly other kinds of flags!

The first submarine may have had a leather top to keep the air in and the water out. The men tried to row underwater. It sank!

Lifeboats are unsinkable. Even if a stormy sea turns one upside down it still floats. That is, if no one pulls the plug out! Do you think there is a plug?

INDEX

Aircraft carriers   53, 63
Barges   10
Barques   28-29
Battleships   36-37, 62
Bulk cargo   40, 41
Canals   10-11, 14-17
Capstan   25
Cargo ships   38-39
Clipper ships   26-27
Cogs   23
Container cargo   40, 41
Coracles   9
Cruisers   52, 53
Cutty Sark   26
Destroyers   52
Dreadnought   36
Dredgers   61
Dug-outs   6
Ferries   48-49
Fire floats   60
Flags   22, 23
Frigates   53
Galleons   22, 24
Galleys   13, 20-21
Hovercraft   51
Hydrofoils   48, 50
Inflatable boats   5
Junks   8
Lateen sail   20
Lifeboats   64

Liners   46-47, 62, 64
Locks   14-15
Longboats   8
Ocean racers   30, 31
Paddle wheels   32-33
Passenger ships   46-47
Pontoons   60
Radar   55
Rafts   7
Reed boats   9
Rigging   28
Sailing ships   7, 18-19, 24, 28
Schooners   28
Sea canals   17
Shipbuilding   44
Sluices   15
Steamships   32
Sternwheeler   33
Submarines   53, 56-57, 64
Tacking   18-19
Tall ships   28-29
Tankers   41-43, 62
Temeraire   62
The Great Britain   34-35
Training ships   28
Trieste   63
Tugs   10
Warships   36, 52-53, 63
Yachts   30
Yawls   30